PRAYER
REFRESH

21 SHORT PRAYERS TO
INCLUDE IN YOUR DAY

A.J. Lykosh

MAKARIOS
PRESS

Esmont, VA

Makarios Press
P.O. Box 28, Esmont, VA 22937

Scripture in NIV unless otherwise stated.

Cover Illustration: Jonelle Lilly
Design: Nate Braxton

ISBN 978-1-956561-03-6

Printed in the United States of America

CONTENTS

Exciting Prayers

INTRODUCTION

Here's a startling proposition: you don't have to completely change your life or your habits or your personality or your social media usage in order to have a good prayer life.

This book introduces a wide variety of short prayers that you can pray in a minute or less, prayers to fit into your day, right where you are.

It is entirely possible that, as you start to practice super short prayers here and there, that you will start to have a greater passion to pray.

In fact, prayer can become almost addictive. (Try it and see!)

When you follow Jesus, and the Holy Spirit abides in you and guides you, you have the guidance to pray as you ought.

Don't start with hours on your knees.

Start with the stray half minutes here and there.

This book offers prayers for the busy and distracted.

In other words: all of us.

FOUNDATIONS

YOU'RE NOT BAD AT PRAYER

In prayer, what do you struggle with, and who do you blame?

All the people I've ever talked to blame themselves for not being as good at prayer as they would wish.

"I'm not consistent enough."

"I can't find my focus."

"I've prayed before and I'm not sure God answered. I think I'm just bad at prayer."

"I don't spend enough time."

Yes, yes, yes, and yes.

I have been there!

One Sunday the worship pastor asked us to close our eyes. Then he asked:

How many of you are really struggling right now—1–3 on the scale of 1–10?

How many are doing okay—4–7 on the scale of 1–10?

How many of you are really doing well, like an 8–10?

It's easy to forget that the people who sit around us are not in the same place we are. And where we are now may not be where we are next week. Yet no matter where we are, we all worship together.

Isn't that powerful? Such a good reminder that all around

us some people are struggling, or doing okay, or doing great. We're in different places.

But what if we change that question a bit and say, "Where are you, on a scale of 1–10, in terms of prayer?"

What would you say?

Even highly motivated pray-ers, in your church or in your life, who you would imagine *really* have their act together ... still don't feel like they do.

The most prayer-ful woman at my church, when asked about prayer, said, "Oh, I'm no expert."

And I thought: *If you're no expert, what hope is there for the rest of us?!*

So if you feel like you're not very good at prayer—join the club!

Later I was talking about this with my prayer mentor, Bob Perry.

He said something that shocked me.

I believe every believer is a 10 in prayer, from the Father's perspective. From the very beginning, he would have ranked me as a 10. Because prayer isn't a matter of performance, but it comes from the heart.

Because you are God's child, he likes you.

I am not a perfect parent. But when one of my sons walks in and says, "I'm home!" and then goes off to shower or study, I don't feel angry that he didn't spend more time with me.

I'm happy that my son greeted me! I'm happy that he's home and safe and in my life!

I think God, too, delights in our small hellos, that he is entirely thrilled every time we acknowledge his presence in our lives.

So here's the answer to, "Just how good at prayer are you?" You're a 10.

You always were, and you always will be.

FOUNDATIONS   7

DON'T CLEAN
YOURSELF UP FIRST

My Sunday school class once had a vigorous discussion about how we are supposed to come to God.

One person suggested, "It's good not to come to God with a whiny spirit."

Another person said, "I totally disagree. You can't lie to God, and so you might as well come. He knows how you're doing anyway, so you might as well not filter yourself, and come without pretense, or with some false posture. If I'm grumpy, I come, even though I'm grumpy."

What do you think about this?

Since God is *El Elyon*, the Most High God, it would seem prudent to treat him with the utmost respect.

Except that when Jesus taught us to pray, he didn't teach us to start with "El Elyon, Most High God."

He taught us to pray, starting with "Our Father."

Except even *Father* isn't quite right.

The word translated "Father," *Abba* in the Aramaic, is less formal.

Jesus taught us to pray starting with "Daddy."

That's a word that young children use, a word of trust and

closeness.

A good daddy knows his children. He doesn't ignore his children when they are pouting or angry. He doesn't turn his back on them, waiting for the children to get their act together so they will be worthy of his time.

No. A good daddy cares for, comforts, and corrects his children.

When we come to God in grumpiness, God gently corrects. He soothes. He redirects. He offers a way forward.

And all of this without condemnation.

One of the most amazing pictures in the entire scripture is Jesus' story of the prodigal son.

When the prodigal son comes to his senses and realizes that he should return to his daddy, he didn't have to first earn back the money he'd lost, or buy himself fine clothes so his daddy wouldn't be embarrassed.

He simply had to go home. He had to repent, to turn back to his daddy.

In this case, he literally returned to his daddy's house.

Dr. Pete Carter, in *Unwrapping Lazarus*, pointed out that yes, we need to recognize our sin and have a contrite heart. But our identity isn't found in our past.

The prodigal thought of himself as a servant, looking for a better master.

But the prodigal's identity was in his bloodline, not his behavior. "He did not fully understand just how full of grace his father was; how willing to forgive and restore. He did not understand that his restoration was in his father's hands not his own."[1]

So good!

May we fully enter in to our identity as sons and daughters of God.

Even if we come dirty and downcast, may we come, so that

we may grasp hold of our complete inheritance. May we take off the bindings of slavery and servanthood, and rejoice to be God's beloved children.

So come to God as you are.

No prepping required.

FOUNDATION 3

DOES PRAYER REALLY MAKE A DIFFERENCE?

D.A. Carson, in *Praying the Prayers of Paul*, talks about two ways that Christians can fall into error with their prayers.

On the one side, we might fall into a sort of fatalism disguised as sovereignty—"What God wills will happen."

The Muslim prayer, "Inshallah," or "If God wills," is an example of this kind of fatalism. People live in resignation that events will play out, without any expectation that what humans do or ask will make a difference.

On the other side, we might fall into a sort of absolute assurance that whatever we pray for, so long as we have enough faith, will happen.

Then, if a prayer isn't answered as expected, that's the fault of either the pray-er or the one being prayed for. If we pray for healing and the person is not healed, the healing failed because someone didn't have enough faith.

Thus we either give ourselves no hope that prayer makes a difference, or too much credit (and too much blame) that prayer makes a difference.

But neither one of these is correct.

God is not a fatalistic God who doesn't hear and respond to

the prayers of his people.

The record of the scripture is that people speak with God and, as a result, God changes the course of his action. For example, in Exodus 32, when the Israelites fell into sin, God was determined to wipe them out. He said to Moses, "Now leave me alone so that my anger may burn against them and that I may destroy them. Then I will make you into a great nation."

But Moses sought the favor of the Lord his God. "Lord," he said, "why should your anger burn against your people, whom you brought out of Egypt with great power and a mighty hand? Why should the Egyptians say, 'It was with evil intent that he brought them out, to kill them in the mountains and to wipe them off the face of the earth'? Turn from your fierce anger; relent and do not bring disaster on your people. Remember your servants Abraham, Isaac and Israel, to whom you swore by your own self: 'I will make your descendants as numerous as the stars in the sky and I will give your descendants all this land I promised them, and it will be their inheritance forever.'"

Deuteronomy tells us, "Then the Lord relented and did not bring on his people the disaster he had threatened."[2]

Moses' prayer appealed to God's character, his mercy to forgive their offenses. He reminded God of his plans to bring Israel through the desert. And Moses persuaded God.

So one man's prayers can make a difference.

On the other hand, God is the Maker of the Universe, and as he points out powerfully to Job, man cannot understand all the ways of God.

When we pray, we don't know the whole picture. So we might not get what we ask for, even if we ask in faith.

God is both sovereign and a prayer-hearing, prayer-answering God.

When we pray, we pray in the place between hopeless

fatalism and guilt that we didn't pray enough.

Our prayers make a difference, but not necessarily in the ways that we expect.

FOUNDATION 4

TWO TYPES OF
THE WORD OF GOD

In Hebrews 4:12 we read, "For the *word* of God is alive and active. Sharper than any double-edged sword, it penetrates even to dividing soul and spirit, joints and marrow; it judges the thoughts and attitudes of the heart."

The Greek for "word" here is *logos*, meaning the written word of God, the Bible that you hold in your hand. That word is powerful, discerning your thoughts and intentions.

But here's something surprising.

In the famous passage of the armor of God, we read, "Take the helmet of salvation and the sword of the Spirit, which is the *word* of God."³

Here the Greek for "word" is not *logos*.

The Bible is not the sword of the Spirit.

Rather, the Greek here is *rhema*, the spoken, living word of God that moves on the heart.

Have you ever felt downcast and discouraged or under attack and had a worship song come to mind that lifted your spirits and pushed back the darkness?

That's an example of a *rhema* word of God, the sword of the Spirit.

Have you had a frustrating day and had a fragment of scripture cross your mind? Again, that was a *rhema* word of God, the sword of the Spirit. In this case, a *rhema* taken from the *logos*.

Sometimes *rhema* words might seem like common sense.

There was one time that I had been gloomy for a few days. Everywhere I turned, I seemed to see another example of failure.

My sister was praying for me over the phone, and while she did so, I put a few books away. I came across one of the boys' schoolbooks, a timeline book. All I needed to do was add preprinted stickers to it, but I hadn't touched it for four and a half years. Failure.

This thought then flashed across my mind: *Not everyone does everything in every season. You yourself, Amy, have no timeline book, and you have never thought yourself a failure in life because you don't.*

Ah. True. A *rhema* word of God.

Some *rhema* words are kind and comforting. Some are truth in the midst of spiraling thoughts.

God gives you the words you need: words of life that spring to mind unexpectedly; scripture verses; worship songs; the memory of a conversation that blessed you.

Our weapon is not just the printed word of God, but all the ways that God is speaking to us.

Praise the God who always gives more!

OUTSTANDING PRAYERS

PRAYER REFRESH 1

HOW TO HEAR GOD'S VOICE

Jesus' sheep hear his voice. This includes you.

If you ask God, "What is one thing you would like me to know today?" would you expect to hear from God?

It's an interesting question!

For years, I wasn't sure that I could hear from God.

But that left me feeling uneasy about certain scriptures, like when Jesus said,

"My sheep hear my voice, and I know them, and they follow me."[4]

Jesus didn't leave any wiggle room there. His sheep hear his voice. Period.

It's not a conditional statement.

Steve Znachko preached a message that had such a beautiful summary of hearing from God.

Here's the truth: God speaks to me and he speaks to you.

In John 16, he promises to guide you in all truth.

In Acts 1:8, he promises to give you power.

In Acts 5, he promises to be witnesses to things you can never experience unless he tells you about them.

In Acts 7, he reveals his glory to you.
In Acts 13, he promises to fill you.
In Luke 10, he brings you rejoicing.
In Luke 12, he's your teacher.
In Romans 5, he pours out the love of God directly into
your heart.
In John 14, he helps you remember who he is.
In Galatians 3:3, he promises to complete what he's already
started in you.
In Romans 2, he circumcises your heart.
And in Romans 8 he says, "I'm your very life."
You are a child of God, and he can't wait to speak to you. That's
just an absolute truth. Walk in that truth.[5]

Jesus' voice doesn't boom out like a radio broadcast from heaven.

Instead, when God speaks, it mostly sounds like our own thoughts, spontaneous ideas flitting through the mind.

Not sure what his voice sounds like?

Expect that what you hear from God will be more kind, more loving, more gentle, more full of grace, more funny, and more enjoyable than you could possibly imagine.

Refresh

If you tell yourself you can't hear from God, that's a lie. Read this prayer aloud.

Lord, stop the mouth of the liar. I cut myself free from the lie that I cannot hear, and I thank you, Jesus, that I am your sheep, and you say that your sheep hear your voice. As Jesus helped deaf men to hear while he walked this earth, please bless my deaf ears that I may hear from you.

Thank you that you are trustworthy, and that my ability to hear doesn't depend on my goodness, but is a gift from you.

Going Forward

As you experiment with hearing God's voice, to begin with, you can ask God questions like these:

Lord, what are you saying to me?

What would you like me to know?

What question would you like to answer?

Be excited to experiment!

And here's a hint to be able to hear more clearly: do what you love.

If you're a musician, ask God to speak, and then play your instrument or sing.

If you're an athlete, ask God to speak, and then run (or ski or tackle or whatever you do).

If you're an artist, ask God to speak, and then work in your favorite medium.

One of my artist friends was trying to hear God's voice, and he kept hearing more rules as he prayed.

Which is not *horrible*, but it's not grace and peace, either.

I asked him to draw for one minute. He grudgingly agreed.

And at the end of the minute, he said, "I think I heard that God is pleased with me?"

Yes. Exactly.

God is pleased with you.

The voice of God: more loving than you could possibly imagine.

PRAYER REFRESH 2

THE DISCIPLES ASKED JESUS TO TEACH THEM ONE THING

If we ask Jesus to teach us to pray, he will!

The disciples walked around with Jesus every day. They heard his teaching and saw his miracles.

And with all of that connection, they still asked Jesus to teach them one specific thing: "Lord, teach us to pray."[6]

They didn't say, "Teach us to preach." Perhaps that was more intuitive!

As Chris Travis points out in *InSignificant*, Jesus didn't say, "There's nothing to know. Just go talk to God."[7]

Instead, he taught them.

Because prayer is not easy!

And, sure, on some level, prayer is easy, because you *can* just talk to God.

But on every other level, prayer isn't easy.

It's not easy because when we speak to people, we can see with our eyes, and hear with our ears. We have immediate, obvious feedback.

It's not easy because we're distracted by the rest of life.

It's not easy because we have an adversary who seeks to steal, kill, and destroy, who actively works to prevent the good gifts of God things that bring life and health ... things like prayer.

So if you struggle with prayer, you're in good company. We're all learning every day.

But God the Father delights in you, in whatever halting, uncomfortable prayers you offer.

And just as Jesus taught the disciples, he also teaches us. Isn't that beautiful?

Refresh

Make the same request that the disciples did.
Lord, teach me to pray!

Going Forward

This is a request that Jesus loves to answer. In the chapters to come, we'll look at some aspects of the Lord's prayer, but you can ask, *Lord, teach me to pray* as often as you want for the rest of your life.

PRAYER REFRESH 3

SEEING THE LORD'S PRAYER WITH NEW EYES

When you pray, pray for God's will to be done.

Chris Travis writes in *Insignificant* about the two years he spent in the worst public middle school in New York. His wife was threatened. He was robbed repeatedly. He struggled with a lack of appreciation, the absolute absence of respect, and what it looked like to do a job with no significance.

The students had no desire to hear what he was teaching, and test scores didn't rise.

He tried to be obedient. He tried to survive.

He spent a lot of time in the Lord's prayer, the prayer Jesus used to teach his disciples how to pray.

Matthew 6:9–13 reads:

This, then, is how you should pray: Our Father in heaven, hallowed be your name, your kingdom come, your will be done, on earth as it is in heaven. Give us today our daily bread. And forgive us our debts, as we also have forgiven our debtors. And lead us not into temptation, but deliver us from the evil one.

Chris learned that first he needed to "align with God's will ... recognizing who God is, praising him, and submitting to his will."

In fact, that's half the prayer! Look at it! Hallowed be *your* name. *Your* kingdom come. *Your* will be done, on earth as it is in heaven.

"Trying to get God to do our will is small and lonely. Asking God to sweep us up into his will, to give us what we need so we can do what he wants—this leads to a life that matters."

Pursue God's will. For Chris, his prayers gradually changed from, "I can't do this anymore. I need a break. Please make my kids behave," to "Father, you want my students to learn and feel safe in my room even more than I do. Show me how to lead them."

This is a prayer of relationship, a prayer of dependence.

Refresh

Pray for the Lord's will.

Father, I glorify your name. I ask that your purposes would go forward on this planet. May I be faithful this day to walk in your ways and bring your will in the places where I live and serve. May I be right before you. Provide. Protect my relationships. May I not be ensnared by the world, but resist all the fiery darts of the evil one. You are the only wise God, and to you belongs all praise.

Going Forward

Observe the language you use in prayer in the days to come. Are you praying for God to do your will, or asking God to use you in his will?

May the Father's blessing be upon you this day. May he show you more of his ways, and may you draw closer to him.

PRAYER REFRESH 4

PRAY THE DETAILS

Look at the creation—from subatomic particles
on up, it's all details. God cares about the
details in your life, so pray for them.

Some years ago, my family was living in tight quarters, with most of our worldly goods in storage. My son asked to read *Greek Myths*. It had been on a shelf until recently, but when I couldn't find it, I realized that I must have packed it up, thinking no one looked at it.

Over the next few weeks, my son mentioned that book several more times. I felt bad, but there wasn't really much I could do. I had certainly not labeled the boxes in storage with lists of individual titles, and I didn't remember packing the book, let alone have any idea where in the crowded storage space I had put the box.

But I finally decided I could at least try, so I made my way into the precarious depths of storage. I had looked in a few boxes without success, and finally, surrounded by boxes, I sat back and closed my eyes for a second, just to be at peace, alone. I was weary and discouraged, and I had no idea how to grant my son this small wish.

My head must have tipped back, because when I opened my eyes, they rested for a second on a box. And I *knew* that was the box with *Greek Myths*.

The wonder of that moment brought tears to my eyes for weeks afterwards. It was such a little thing, just a single book among thousands, just a small request from a young boy. Nothing important or spiritually uplifting or necessary. If anything it was going in the wrong direction! A picture book about false gods!

But to me it felt like the palpable presence of God was there, showing me that he sustains his children, that he grants us even the little gifts.

James said it best, of course: "Every good gift and every perfect gift is from above."[8]

Dr. Jane Glenchur pointed out that although some people think we should reserve our prayers for great matters, the reality of Creation shows that God gives incredible attention to detail! It's all details![9]

So don't reserve prayers just for big things. Pray about *everything.*

The Amplified Version of I Peter 5:7 says, "Casting the whole of your care [all your anxieties, all your worries, all your concerns, once and for all] on Him, for He cares for you affectionately and cares about you watchfully."

"All your concerns" is a pretty low bar. This is not for big concerns only. It could be as small as not knowing what to make for dinner with the random ingredients in your pantry. "Lord, what should I make for dinner?"

One of my friends said that, in the season after her unwanted divorce, when she found it hard to get out of bed, she would pray, "Let me make my bed today. Let me do the laundry."

All day long, she would ask, "Help me do the next thing," or "what should I do about ____?"

Quick prayers, easy to pray, and easy to move on. And God was with her.

God in the details.

Refresh

Find a detail in your day that you wouldn't normally think to pray about, and talk to God about it.

Thank you, Jesus, that you taught us to pray, "Give us this day our daily bread." Thank you that you care about the details.

Lord, show me the next thing I'm supposed to do.

Going Forward

Start to remember to go to God with the details. Less worry, more prayer!

Your Father in heaven affectionately cares for you. The Lord bless you with his presence and his love. He will provide for you and protect you.

Grace and peace to you.

PRAYER REFRESH 5

PRAYER OF REPENTANCE

As a follower of Jesus, you are free from sin. Should you ever find yourself falling into sin, turn from it immediately and walk again in newness of life.

Romans teaches that those who have peace with God are dead to sin and should not live any longer in it.

So don't allow sin to rule in your mortal body, to make you obey its desires. Nor should you present your limbs and organs to sin to be used for its wicked purposes. Rather, present yourselves to God, as people alive from the dead, and your limbs and organs to God, to be used for the righteous purposes of his covenant. Sin won't actually rule over you, you see, since you are not under law but under grace.[10]

It's sort of like we used to be fish, swimming in the ocean water of sin. The water was our natural state.

Then we died, and were raised to new life. But our new life starts as new creatures, like mice, breathing the air of righteousness.

A mouse might fall into the ocean by accident, but it's not home any longer.

So if you're intentionally sinning and blowing it off, telling yourself something like, "We all sin all the time"—wrong! Stop! You're free to walk in righteousness!

Don't ever choose sin.

In the novel *Anne of Green Gables*, Anne says at one point, "Isn't it nice to think that tomorrow is a new day with no mistakes in it yet?"

As a child, I liked that idea.

As a young parent, I grew to hate that quote, because if I made a mistake at 7:30am—which was not uncommon—it was so tremendously long until the next day began with a fresh start.

It took me a few years to realize that, if a person can come to Jesus for the first time, without waiting for a brand new morning, I, too, could come to Jesus at any time of the day, have all the sins and mistakes washed away, and start afresh. Every minute, if I needed to!

What a relief, to find that, even if a day began badly, it could always be redeemed. In a few moments all the yuckiness could be washed away.

And isn't it interesting: in the Lord's prayer, the request right after the prayer for daily bread is a plea to "forgive us our debts, as we forgive our debtors."

The word "debts" is a word that means "that which is owed; that which is legally due."

Metaphorically, it can mean sin. But even apart from a metaphor: God is due all honor and glory. When we don't give him what we owe, we become debtors.

Every day may we be forgiven for not giving what is due.

This is life: intentional obedience. Sometimes failure. Seeking forgiveness. Starting anew.

You always have a choice. Choose well.

Refresh

Are you consciously in sin? Ask God, and see if he brings anything to mind. Then pray this prayer.

Lord God, you are worthy of all praise and glory. You know my inmost thoughts. I repent and turn away from any and all words, thoughts, and deeds that are not of you. I renounce any ways that I may have been in agreement with the evil one. I ask your forgiveness and claim the blood of Christ as my covering. Look on me with his righteousness and not my own.

As I go forward, I ask that you would make me attentive to your guidance. Whenever I get off track, please show me, so that I can turn again and walk in grace and peace.

And now, Lord God, I ask that you would show me specific ways that I can be obedient today. Please let me be a good ambassador for your kingdom, and may your love flow through me to this hurting world.

I thank you that you gave us the perfect example of Jesus, and I ask that I would follow Him faithfully.

I ask these things in the name of Jesus, the faithful and true. Amen.

Going Forward

Walk in obedience this day. Should you fail to walk in Christ's footsteps, confess your sin immediately, seek forgiveness as needed, and move on, washed in the blood of Christ.

Jesus sends us a helper, the Holy Spirit, our advantage. Receive God's love ... and then give his love.

PRAYER REFRESH 6

WEEDING PRAYER

We are commanded to forgive, as we have been
forgiven. If you're not yet ready to forgive,
you can ask for the will to forgive, and pray a
blessing over the one you need to forgive.

Frederick Buechner, in *Wishful Thinking*, defines
forgiveness thus:

*To forgive somebody is to say one way or another, "You have
done something unspeakable, and by all rights I should call it quits
between us. Both my pride and my principles (q.v.) demand no less.
However, although I make no guarantees that I will be able to forget
what you've done, and though we may both carry the scars for life, I
refuse to let it stand between us. I still want you for my friend.*

*To accept forgiveness means to admit that you've done something
unspeakable that needs to be forgiven, and thus both parties must
swallow the same thing: their pride.*

*This seems to explain what Jesus means when he says to God,
"Forgive us our trespasses as we forgive those who trespass against
us." Jesus is not saying that God's forgiveness is conditional upon
our forgiving others. In the first place, forgiveness that's conditional*

isn't really forgiveness at all, just Fair Warning; and in the second place, our unforgivingness is among those things about us which we need to have God forgive us most. What Jesus apparently is saying is that the pride which keeps us from forgiving is the same pride which keeps us from accepting forgiveness, and will God please help us do something about it.

When somebody you've wronged forgives you, you're spared the dull and self-diminishing throb of a guilty conscience.

When you forgive somebody who has wronged you, you're spared the dismal corrosion of bitterness and wounded pride.

For both parties, forgiveness means the freedom again to be at peace inside their own skins and to be glad in each other's presence.

Sometimes forgiveness comes, supernaturally and totally. Corrie ten Boom had a beloved sister die in a Nazi concentration camp. After the war, Corrie toured the world, speaking about forgiveness.

One night, one of the most cruel of the Nazi prison guards greeted her after her talk and said, "It is true! I was a horrible sinner, but God has washed my sins away! And now I ask you to forgive me, too." And he stuck out his hand to shake hers.

Corrie writes of how, in her own strength, she had no ability to forgive. She could only see her beloved sister suffering under this man. But she remembered that forgiveness is not an emotion, but an act of the will. And she prayed, "Jesus, help me!" She realized that at least she could shake his hand. She had the physical mobility for that.

And so woodenly, mechanically, I thrust my hand into the one stretched out to meet me. And as I did, an incredible thing took place. The current started in my shoulder, raced down my arm, sprang into our joined hands. And then this healing warmth seemed to flood my whole being, bringing tears to my eyes.

"I forgive you, brother!" I cried. "With all my heart."

For a long moment we grasped each other's hands, the former

guard and the former prisoner. I had never known God's love so
intensely, as I did then. But even so, I realized it was not my love. I
had tried, and did not have the power. It was the power of the Holy
Spirit as recorded in Romans 5:5, "... because the love of God is shed
abroad in our hearts by the Holy Ghost which is given unto us."[11]

Such a beautiful story.

But not all forgiveness is so instantaneous and miraculous.

I don't know if you have ever had to forgive someone for
something major. I think of one time in my life, where I
happily forgave the person one day. And the next day, my
thoughts started to dwell on the same sin again. So I forgave a
second time. Until later that day, when I forgave a third time.

This went on for months.

Corrie ten Boom tells of a similar situation in her own life.
She, too, kept forgiving, again and again.

Finally she asked God about this, because it bothered her to
revisit the same situation over and over. And she remembered
Paul's words in Ephesians 6: "after you have come to a
standstill, still stand your ground."

She realized that she had come to a standstill, but she could
still stand firm.

In Matthew 18, Peter asks Jesus how many times he is
to forgive, and Jesus replies with a radically large number.
Depending on the translation: 77 times, or 70 times 7.

Usually I read that number as separate offenses—a person
keeps on sinning against you.

In that case, even Peter's initial suggestion of seven times
is a bit over-the-top. I mean, if a friend stood me up once,
that's not cool. But once is understandable—maybe the phone
notification was accidentally set for 4am instead of 4pm.
Things happen.

But imagine blithely going off to meet that friend for lunch,
and you get stood up a second time. And a third time. And

a fourth time. And a fifth time. And a sixth time. And a seventh time.

Peter was already being generous, suggesting seven times. And Jesus ups the ante so much.

But sometimes I wonder if part of forgiveness, for a really hard thing, is that we have to keep forgiving, over and over, as our mind keeps returning to the already forgiven offense.

And yet the call remains: forgive.

Refresh

Ask God if you have anyone to forgive.

Whoever comes to mind, no matter how small and insignificant the event, forgive the person.

If you can't in yourself, pray for the will to be able to forgive. Then forgive as an act of obedience to the direct command of God.

Finally, pray a blessing over the offender: "Love your enemies, bless them that curse you, do good to them that hate you, and pray for them which despitefully use you, and persecute you."

Lord God, I thank you that you offer me forgiveness, and that you remember my sins no more. Thank you for Hebrews 12:15, that says, "See to it that no one falls short of the grace of God and that no bitter root grows up to cause trouble and defile many." I don't want any bitter root growing in me!

Please bring to mind anyone I haven't forgiven.

Remembering that experience is painful, Lord God. I want to be obedient. Please show me how to forgive.

I ask that you would pour out blessings on that person.

Going Forward

Some people recommend asking God nightly: "Is there

anything that needs to be cut off of my from this day?"

Whenever you notice bitterness or unforgiveness sprouting, uproot it, as often as necessary.

Because of the work of Jesus on the cross, you are forgiven. Now go and do likewise.

PRAYER REFRESH 7

PRAYER OF PROTECTION

**Jesus taught us to pray, "Deliver us from evil"
or "deliver us from the evil one." Clothe yourself
and your family in the armor of God.**

My college mentor Connie Anderson told about an interaction with a seasoned overseas missionary.

"You need to daily pray protection over yourself and your family."

I put that in a category in my head named, "Things I should do, but don't, and feel rather guilty about."

My husband and I have always had an apostolic gifting to plant, or encourage those who are planting, new works of God in areas with little witness. Soon the opposition of the enemy became nearly unbearable.

We began to take our missionary's advice seriously, and began praying together daily with a commitment to protect ourselves in prayer from the enemy.

Peter describes the evil one. "Be alert and of sober mind. Your enemy the devil prowls around like a roaring lion *looking for someone to devour.*"[12]

Do you feel like your children are being devoured? Would you like that to stop?

Or can you imagine it happening, and you'd prefer to make
sure it doesn't happen?

Paul gives some familiar instructions in Ephesians 6:10–17.

*Finally, be strong in the Lord and in his mighty power. Put on
the full armor of God, so that you can take your stand against the
devil's schemes. For our struggle is not against flesh and blood, but
against the rulers, against the authorities, against the powers of this
dark world and against the spiritual forces of evil in the heavenly
realms. Therefore put on the full armor of God, so that when the
day of evil comes, you may be able to stand your ground, and
after you have done everything, to stand. Stand firm then, with
the belt of truth buckled around your waist, with the breastplate of
righteousness in place, and with your feet fitted with the readiness
that comes from the gospel of peace. In addition to all this, take up
the shield of faith, with which you can extinguish all the flaming
arrows of the evil one. Take the helmet of salvation and the sword of
the Spirit, which is the word of God.*

*And pray in the Spirit on all occasions with all kinds of prayers
and requests. With this in mind, be alert and always keep on
praying for all the Lord's people.*

Vic Black tells about a vision where he popped his
head up in the middle of a field. On one side were all the
demons. Horrible!

On the other side were the angelic heavenly host.

And there was his head poking up in the middle of the field.

Then God the Father caught his eye. And God looked at Vic
with love, but maybe a bit of concern, too, and said, "Where is
your armor?!"

The vision is a bit humorous. You can imagine it playing
out like a cartoon: orcs and goblins on one side, gorgeous holy
warriors on the other side.

And in the middle, a man clad in long-johns.

Oops!

Why would anyone go into battle without armor?

We are in a battle! So put on your armor.

Which all sounds well and good. But what does it look like, practically?

Francis MacNutt says of prayer, "Everyone gets to play."

Husbands and wives together, a single parent alone, parents with children, praying mothers ... everyone gets to play.

For Connie, she and her husband kneel at the couch each morning. Together, they ask the Lord for protection over their day. Her husband lines up the family members in his head, and as he prays, he imagines dressing each one of them in the piece of armor as he prays it out loud.

As Connie said, "At first this prayer time was awkward. Over time it became normal. Now its awkward if we don't do it. If we miss a day, we usually can tell by about 3 o'clock in the afternoon. We'll look at each other and say, 'Oh! We didn't pray today.'"

How long does it take to pray through putting on the armor of God?

It can be less than twenty seconds per person.

This prayer is not meant to be a really long part of the day. Adding this should not require a major shift in your daily schedule.

But here is why this is so important.

When lions hunt, they don't take down the strongest of the herd.

They bring down the weakest.

The accuser also goes after the weakest member of the family. If you are seeking to glorify God in your life, the accuser focuses on the place he can gain the most agency. Often this is the marriage. Often this is the children.

Resist this in the authority Jesus gives you.

Refresh

Pray to clothe yourself with the armor of God.

Lord, I put on the breastplate of righteousness, the belt of truth, the shoes fitted with the preparation of the gospel of peace, the helmet of salvation, and I take up the sword of the Spirit and the shield of faith.

Going Forward

Dress yourself and your family in the armor of God every day. Picture each person in your mind—it's fine if the picture is blurry or not perfectly clear.

You are God's workmanship. You are his handiwork. You are his masterpiece.

Walk in victory.

GROWING PRAYERS

PRAYER REFRESH 8

ONE SENTENCE TO START THE DAY PRAYER

Start your day with a one sentence prayer, such as
"What would you have me do today?"

Psalm 63, a Psalm of David, begins with a reminder of
seeking God early.
O God, You are my God;
Early will I seek You;
My soul thirsts for You;
My flesh longs for You
In a dry and thirsty land
Where there is no water.
Some years ago, I asked the Lord first thing in the morning,
"What would you have me do today?" Or, as Corrie ten Boom
would say, "Can you use me in some way?"
One Sunday I had a strong impulse to buy flowers for an
acquaintance. I didn't know her well, but I knew her well
enough to know where she lived. All through church, the
impression remained strong, so as soon as I could get away
after lunch, I bought a bouquet and drove over to her house.
On the way I called to let her know I was stopping by.

The call went to voice mail.

I wasn't expecting that. I had thought she would be there. I left an awkward message like, "This is Amy. I'm bringing something by."

Then I hoped she would have returned in the few minutes before I got to her house.

But she hadn't.

Which left me with a dilemma. It was early March in Colorado, and I felt weird leaving a bouquet by her condo door. Would the flowers even survive? Would a neighbor walk away with them?

What's the right protocol when you do what you think you're supposed to, but it looks nothing like what you expect?

In the end, I figured that I had the bouquet, and I had done what I felt I was supposed to do, so I left the flowers and drove home, with a sense of confusion and at least a bit of a sense of futility.

So I was amazed a few hours later when I got a call. My acquaintance had been skiing, and had no cell service. So she walked up to her door, without having listened to my message, and found flowers waiting.

She said, "On Valentine's Day a few weeks ago, I said to God, 'You know, God, one of the things that I hate about being single is that no one brings me flowers.' And then I got home, and there were flowers waiting for me! You were God's answer to my prayer! God sees me!"

And from that day on, this acquaintance became one of my dear friends.

That's an amazing story, and I love it.

But that's also the most dramatic example of prompting I remember. There were a few other small promptings, but nothing quite so exciting.

Truth be told, I eventually stopped praying this prayer. It's

awesome to have an amazing story, but it's not quite so fun
when you pray, day after day, and hear little.

A few years after I had stopped praying this prayer, I was
talking about this experience with a mentor. She chuckled
a little and said, "Your prayer is about *doing*. What if God
didn't have anything for you to *do*? What if He just wanted
to *be* with you? What if you changed this prayer to, 'What
adventure do you have for us today?' And then move forward,
knowing that you'll do it together?"

I like that, too.

Well-known pastor A.W. Tozer had a pianist who served
for thirty years. That woman lived to be 100, and in the week
before her death, she said to a pastor and his wife, "Every day
I ask God, 'Give me a clean heart, a wise heart, a deep heart.'"

That, too, is a lovely prayer.

Healing prayer minister Judith MacNutt said that she and her
husband pray for the filling of the Holy Spirit for each other
every day.

How beautiful.

Refresh

Pick the prayer that most resonates with you, and pray it in
the morning.

- What would you have me do today?
- Can you use me in some way?
- What adventure do you have for me today?
- Give me a clean heart, a wise heart, a deep heart.
- Fill me this day with the Holy Spirit.

Be on the lookout for ways that God answers!

*Lord, what adventure do you have for me today? Let me be ready
and alert. Thank you that you are with me.*

Going Forward

Put a reminder of this prayer where you will see it every day when you first wake up, and start to say this prayer at the start of every day. Whether it's a post-it on your night stand or mirror, a reminder on your phone, a notecard resting on top of your underwear—use a simple prompt to start a new prayer habit.

The Lord bless you with his presence. You will be filled as you hunger and thirst.

PRAYER REFRESH 9

THE VISITING PRAYER

**Whenever you visit someone, pray a
blessing over your conversation.**

I was out for an afternoon with one of my dear friends,
and the subject turned to prayer. I mentioned that I
tried to remember to say, "Lord, bless our conversation"
before visiting.

And she said, "Oh, I pray, 'Let the words of my mouth and
the meditation of my heart be acceptable in your sight, O
Lord, my rock and my redeemer.'"[13]

Which I preferred, because it uses scripture.

Refresh

If you visit with someone today, pray this prayer.

Before church, or a meeting with friends. Before you interact
with family members or neighbors. Before you head into work or
the grocery store.

If you will talk to someone else, pray beforehand.

*O, Lord, as I meet with others this day, let the words of my mouth
and the meditation of my heart be acceptable in your sight, O Lord,*

my rock and my redeemer. Thank you that you give me sisters and brothers on the journey. I bless your name.

Going Forward

Pray this prayer before every visit, and see how your conversations tend to be more uplifting and satisfying.

You are royally blessed and highly favored.

PRAYER REFRESH 10
THE GUARANTEED PRAYER

God always gives wisdom. Ask for it!

I was working on a project once, and I needed to design a
simple part.

Except a clear design had eluded me. I had started thinking
about a design in October, and by March, I was still
futzing with it.

Finally I said, "Lord! I am so sick of thinking about this
silly design! I want my mind to be able to think about other
things! Please give me wisdom!"

And within fifteen seconds, the needed design popped into
my mind, with all the elegance and precision that I would
expect from the Maker of the Universe.

Clearly it was silly of me not to ask for wisdom for almost
half a year, because asking for wisdom is one of the most
exciting prayers ever.

Where could you use wisdom today?

Refresh

Ask for wisdom, and you'll get it!

Lord, James 1 says, "If any of you lacks wisdom, let him ask God, who gives generously to all without reproach, and it will be given him. But let him ask in faith, with no doubting, for the one who doubts is like a wave of the sea that is driven and tossed by the wind. For that person must not suppose that he will receive anything from the Lord; he is a double-minded man, unstable in all his ways."

Thank you that you promise to give wisdom. Let me ask without doubting.

Please give me wisdom! Thank you, Lord!

Going Forward

Ask for wisdom as often as you need it.

One observation from praying this prayer: sometimes, as with my need for wisdom for the design, the wisdom given proves lasting.

Sometimes, though, I get wisdom for that day, enough to move forward. But then I need to ask for wisdom again.

This happened at one point when my family was trying to think of a name. We spent a few days until we came up with a super exciting name.

But we found out later we couldn't use that name. So we prayed again, and came up with another amazing name! And we were super excited ... until that one didn't work, either.

I'm not sure why we don't immediately get perfect, permanent wisdom every time, but I suspect it has something to do with the need to keep asking—sort of like asking for daily bread.

In my experience, sometimes God gives wisdom in an iterative process. In the end, we can look back and say that we got wisdom when we asked, and had all the wisdom we needed, even if we didn't get the end result wisdom right at the beginning.

Which is to say: if this happens to you, just ask for wisdom again.

May God give you an increase in wisdom, and give you insight on how to bring his solutions to your world.

PRAYER REFRESH 11
PRAYER TO ACCEPT OR RESIST

Sometimes resistance means, "Change course";
sometimes it means "persevere." If you don't know
instantly, you can pray, "If this is from you, I accept it;
if it's not from you, I resist it."

There was a season on the farm where we had a clear vision
of what we wanted to accomplish. And in the course of one
month, all the work, planning, and focus of the previous five
months completely unraveled. The milk cow died. The freezer
broke with two pigs' worth of pork. The new chicks spread
a virus that stopped all our egg-laying hens from ever laying
another egg. The queen bee died and her hive didn't recover.
The neighbor's dog killed dozens of meat chickens right before
it was time to butcher. Bugs wiped out all our vegetables.

I'm not making this up.

It was devastating.

So at the end of this time, when we expected to have crops
and animals and food, and instead had a bunch of death, we
had to stop and re-evaluate and seek the Lord. Were we doing

what we were supposed to?

And both my husband and I felt strongly that we had gotten off track. That as painful as the unraveling was, that God was behind it, and that this was his way to get our attention and say, "Stop running so fast in the wrong direction!"

Sometimes when we're not doing what we're supposed to, the Lord puts roadblocks in our way, to make us change direction.

Another time, several of us were working on a major work project with a very short turnaround. And in that span of three weeks, odd things kept happening: the designer's computer kept locking up, weird accidents, unexpected conversations that quickly turned sour.

Was this a sign to change direction?

No. In this case, as we prayed about it, we felt strongly that these challenges were a form of spiritual attack that we needed to resist.

Praise God for James 4:7: "Submit yourselves therefore to God. Resist the devil, and he will flee from you."

What a promise!

But notice how challenging life can be: a frustration or a thwarting can sometimes be a sign of moving in the wrong direction and a need for change, or the frustration can be from the enemy, as a sign of moving in the right direction and a need for perseverance.

How to tell?

You can *always* ask God for wisdom, of course.

But I also came across a prayer in a book by Isobel Kuhn, a missionary to the Lisu people in western China. She would pray, "If this obstacle be from Thee, Lord, I accept it; but if it be from Satan, I refuse him and all his works in the name of Calvary."

It would, of course, be great if we could always be

completely discerning at every instant. But I love this prayer
because it allows me to simply pray, without having to make
sure that my discernment is clear.

Refresh

For a frustration today, pray this prayer.
*Lord God, if this is from you, I accept it. If it's not from you, I
reject it.*

Going Forward

Remember this short prayer whenever you face an obstacle.
May God grant you his discernment and always a
way forward.

PRAYER REFRESH 12
THE JESUS PRAYER

Blind Bartimaeus called out repeatedly, "Jesus, son of David, have mercy on me!" Sometimes we need to cry out repeatedly, too.

Mark 10 tells the story of Bartimaeus, who sat by the roadside begging.

> *When he heard that Jesus was passing by, he called out, "Jesus, son of David, have mercy on me!"*
> *And when those around him tried to quiet him, he called out all the louder, "Son of David, have mercy on me."*
> *Jesus summoned him, then asked, "What do you want me to do for you?"*
> *"Rabbi, I want to see."*
> *"Go. Your faith has healed you."*[14]

In the Eastern Orthodox Church, they pray "the Jesus prayer," which is similar to the plea of Bartimaeus: "Lord Jesus Christ, son of God, have mercy on me!"

Some versions add a bit to the end: "Lord Jesus Christ, son of God, have mercy on me, a sinner!"

Some people will say this prayer 1000 times a day, as a spiritual discipline.

For me, I don't pray a set number of times, because I suspect I would make this prayer about my works, rather than God's grace.

But clearly Bartimaeus repeated himself. He didn't cry out 1000 times, but did cry out until Jesus responded.

He kept calling, as long as it took.

The first time I prayed the Jesus prayer, I was terribly discouraged. I walked around the block, saying, "Lord Jesus Christ, son of God, have mercy on me."

I said this perhaps 30 times as I walked around my block.

Then I felt equipped again to return to my life.

I needed to cry out more than one time, but I didn't need to cry out for hours.

Sometimes I pray this prayer while walking, with a step for each word.

Sometimes I pray while sitting still, matching my breathing.

I try to think about each of the different statements as I pray.

- Lord: he is the Lord of my life, in control.
- Jesus: the name of the man, meaning "Yahweh saves."
- Christ: the role of the man, meaning "the anointed one, the chosen one, the Messiah, the one who saves the world."
- Son of God: the magnificent one, exalted. (Sometimes I say "Son of David," in which case I think: the one prophesied to come, descended according to the scriptures.)
- Have mercy: show compassion to relieve suffering.
- On me: do this for me—I need it!

Refresh

Pray the Jesus prayer a few times.
Lord Jesus Christ, son of God, have mercy on me.
Lord Jesus Christ, son of God, have mercy on me.
Lord Jesus Christ, son of God, have mercy on me.
Thank you, Lord! Thank you!

Going Forward

Pray this as often as you need to.
You have been redeemed. You have been restored. You have
been bought back by the blood and the sacrifice of the Lord
Jesus Christ.
He is with you.

PRAYER REFRESH 13

SILENT PRAYER

**Some prayer is silence, simply being
in the presence of God. Try it.**

Not all prayers require words.

Psalm 46:10: "He says, 'Be still, and know that I am God;
I will be exalted among the nations, I will be exalted in
the earth.'"

Lamentations 3:26: "It is good that one should wait quietly
for the salvation of the Lord."

Psalm 62:5: "For God alone, O my soul, wait in silence, for
my hope is from him."

Habakkuk 2:20: "But the Lord is in his holy temple; let all
the earth keep silence before him."

I think silence is different than listening, though both
involve being quiet.

Listening is part of communication, and includes an
expectation of an exchange of information.

But with silence, there is simply peace.

Refresh

Spend one minute being silent: quieting your mind, quieting your mouth, not even listening. Just being in presence of the Lord.

Lord, I am here.

Going Forward

Can you find a silent minute every day? Maybe when you're in the bathroom? Or the time before you fall asleep?

Instead of checking your phone or thinking of the next task of the day, try a brief time of silence in the presence of the Lord.

As you wait upon the Lord and his goodness, he will guide, he will speak, and he will provide.

PRAYER REFRESH 14

DECLARATIONS

Some prayers are simply declarations of truth.

Robert Cialdini wrote an entire book, *Pre-suasion*, about how much more effective marketing can be if you set the stage in advance. For example, when a mattress company changed the background on their website to puffy clouds, people purchased their mattresses at a shockingly higher rate. If that's true in the world, where clouds encourage a certain behavior, how much more powerful if you start your day with truth before you go out into the world each day?

- I can do all things through Christ who strengthens me.[15]
- God daily loads me with benefits. He is my salvation.[16]
- I am blessed when I come in and blessed when I go out.[17]
- The joy of the LORD is my strength.[18]
- God has not given me a spirit of fear. He gives me a spirit of power, love, and a sound mind.[19]
- God blesses me abundantly. I always have everything I need, and plenty left over to share with others.[20]
- My ways please the LORD and He makes even my enemies to be at peace with me.[21]

- The Lord is my God! He is mighty to save. He rejoices over me with gladness and singing. I am quieted by His love.[22]
- God redeems my life from the pit. He crowns me with lovingkindness and compassion.[23]
- Christ bore my sins in His own body on the cross and I am healed by His stripes.[24]

Now you might be thinking, as I did initially, *Declarations are well and good, but they aren't really* prayer, *right?*

If anything, these statements feel like the power of positive thinking, with a Christian spin.

And, yes, Romans 12:2 says, "Do not conform to the pattern of this world, but be transformed by the renewing of your mind. Then you will be able to test and approve what God's will is—his good, pleasing and perfect will."

And saying and believing declarations would probably help renew our minds.

But still ... is this really *prayer*? It's not really talking to God, right?

As I've thought about this more, I think that declarations of truth and scripture can be prayer. But rather than people speaking to God, these declarations are more like God speaking to people, and people trying to get to a place of deep belief, rather than just mental assent.

Do I believe that God rejoices over me with gladness and singing?

Or do I (secretly) think God mostly disapproves of me, that I frustrate him a lot of the time?

Do I believe that God blesses me abundantly?

Or do I (occasionally) think about all the financial, relational, or educational disappointments I've had?

Do I know that I have all I need, *and* plenty to share?

Or do I (sometimes) feel like I don't quite have enough, and certainly none to spare?

If God has spoken in his word, who am I to disbelieve?

If God has spoken, and I *do* disbelieve, maybe my prayer needs to begin with hearing what God says and repeating it back to him.

In parenting, if you're not sure a child really understood your instructions, what do you do?

Ask the child to repeat what you just said.

So maybe if we're not sure we're hearing God's words well, we can repeat what he said back to him.

Refresh

Read through this list of declarations out loud, with conviction, as your prayer for today.

- *I can do all things through Christ who strengthens me.*
- *God daily loads me with benefits. He is my salvation.*
- *I am blessed when I come in and blessed when I go out.*
- *The joy of the LORD is my strength.*
- *God has not given me a spirit of fear. He gives me a spirit of power, love, and a sound mind.*
- *God blesses me abundantly. I always have everything I need, and plenty left over to share with others.*
- *My ways please the LORD and He makes even my enemies to be at peace with me.*
- *The Lord is my God! He is mighty to save. He rejoices over me with gladness and singing. I am quieted by His love.*
- *God redeems my life from the pit. He crowns me with lovingkindness and compassion.*
- *Christ bore my sins in His own body on the cross and I am healed by His stripes.*

Going Forward

Did you find any of those declarations more difficult

to believe?

Talk to God about this. "I don't have much joy, let alone enough that it feels like it gives me strength."

Or maybe, "I have no idea what it would feel like to be crowned with lovingkindness and compassion, but I'm pretty sure I don't feel like that."

It's okay to be honest with God!

Whichever sentence stood out to you, try to declare it several times a day. Write it on your mirror. Stick it on your fridge.

Start to get truth into your mind and your heart.

May the Lord go before you and give you his peace.

EXCITING PRAYERS

PRAYERS FOR THE EXCLUDED MIDDLE

The excluded middle sits between the big picture
questions (like salvation and ethics), and the other end
of the spectrum with observable facts (seeds sprout
and yeast rises). This is the space for questions like,
"What about *this* loaf of bread—will it rise?" The Celts
prayed for the excluded middle, and we can, too.

In *The Celtic Way of Evangelism*, George G. Hunter III talked
about "The Flaw of the Excluded Middle."

Religion offers answers to the top level, big picture things,
like salvation and ultimate questions.

At the other extreme are the observable features of the
world, the empirical world. We know that yeast rises, that
seeds sprout, that walking, driving, or flying will transport us
at a generally known speed, in order to reach a destination at
a generally predictable time.

But between these two extremes is the excluded middle.

Yes, we know that, in general, seeds sprout. But what about
this *specific* seed? Will it sprout?

What about this *specific* loaf of bread? Will it rise? Will it cook all the way through?

What about this *specific* trip? Will I walk without twisting an ankle? Will I drive without a traffic jam? Will my flight depart on time?

The excluded middle is uncertain!

And as such, we find in the excluded middle things like luck, the evil eye, shamans, and amulets.

In the West, we don't usually think about praying for the excluded middle.

Perhaps the indigenous cultures around the world have a more clear understanding of what's at play.

Celtic Christians had prayers for all of these daily things, prayers recorded in the *Carmina Gadelica* (*Gaelic Songs*).

Though few of those specific songs apply to my daily life, I love the intention and invitation to pray for the things of the excluded middle.

Refresh

Notice an excluded middle in your life and pray for it today.

From "Prayer for Traveling"
Life be in my speech,
Sense in what I say,
The bloom of cherries on my lips,
Till I come back again.
The love Christ Jesus gave
Be filling every heart for me,
The love Christ Jesus gave
Filling me for every one.

Going Forward

Continue to watch and pray for the excluded middle.

Here are a few more examples from *Carmina Gadelica*.

From "Prayer at Rising"

Bless to me, O God,
Each thing mine eye sees;
Bless to me, O God,
Each sound mine ear hears;
Bless to me, O God,
Each odor that goes to my nostrils;
Bless to me, O God,
Each taste that goes to my lips,
Each note that goes to my song,
Each ray that guides my way,
Each thing that I pursue.

"God's Aid"

God to enfold me,
God to surround me,
God in my speaking,
God in my thinking.

God in my sleeping,
God in my waking,
God in my watching,
God in my hoping.

God in my life,
God in my lips,
God in my soul,
God in my heart.

God in my sufficing,
God in my slumber,
God in mine ever-living soul,
God in mine eternity.

CAR PRAYER

Your car can be a personal prayer pod.

There was one month that I had worked more hours than I ever had in my life. All involved with the project felt both the provision of the Lord in great abundance, but also fatigue, resistance, and frustration.

In the midst of this, I headed up to town for a friend's birthday celebration. I had a 45 minute drive ahead of me, and that particular day I put on the Sons of Korah album *Refuge*, which begins with a gorgeous version of Psalm 94.

As I listened I started crying so hard I wondered if I should pull over. Wailing, screaming, sobbing. Anger over the ways people are wicked, over the ways that Satan is so malicious, over blind eyes and foolish hearts.

I listened to the song six times in a row before I felt ready to let the album move on to the second track.

It wasn't until later that I realized that the times I drive alone are truly a gift.

In my daily life, I share a modest sized home with a number of other people. If I cry, I try to do it quietly, because otherwise someone comes to comfort me, or someone grows upset.

But in the car, alone? I can yell or cry or sing, without someone coming to shush me. It's a personal prayer pod!

A few suggestions, after experimenting with car prayer for some years.

1. Pray out loud.

Because of the number of things that need attention while driving, I've found it helpful to act like I'm on the phone with God, and talk out loud. Otherwise, I end up five miles further down the road, having drifted into random musings on snarky responses to a previous conversation ... and that's not the most uplifting.

2. Listen to scripture.

If you're in a season of such exhaustion that even forming words will be a bit much—and we've all been there—try scripture set to music. I've mentioned Sons of Korah. Some other possibilities: Seeds Family Worship, Sing the Word, Shane and Shane, Randall Goodgame, Marty Goetz.

3. Experiment with more impassioned prayers.

You know how some Psalms sound seriously angry? Like, "Break their teeth! Let them no longer be able to bite and tear!" Most likely, you haven't seen anyone pray like that, because it's so violent it feels almost sinful.

But there are things that are so evil, we should want them to stop with our whole being. "Break the hold of opioid addiction! Stop child sex trafficking! Turn the hearts of men to their wives, and away from digital gratification! May the next generation grow up to serve God's kingdom! Stop those who behead their enemies!"

Since much of my prayer life sounds like a sedate prayer meeting, more impassioned prayers push me out of the comfortable familiar.

And if you haven't ever really screamed in anger over the ways that the enemy entices people to waste their lives ... alone time in the car offers an opportunity for that.

4. Pray for the specific needs you pass. A few examples:

- Pray for the homeless—so many are mentally ill and without a social network.
- Pray for emergency vehicles, those obvious attention-grabbers. Pray for the people who need the ambulance or the fire truck. And pray for the families who have just had their lives upended in small or large ways.
- Pray for the police car and the one pulled over. A ticket can be more than a ticket. Pray for peace.
- Pray for the churches you go by: that they would be places of truth and restoration, that they would be accurate pictures of God to the world.

   When our pastor's family first came to town, a Christian doctor met the pastor's wife at one point. He said, "Oh! I know where your church is! I pray for that church when I drive past!"
   She said, "I immediately started crying that this man that I had never met prayed for us."

The world is hungry for your prayers.

Refresh

Try a car prayer today.
Lord God, thank you that you hear me wherever I am. I pray for protection as I drive. I pray that you would set a watch before my

lips. Be with the people on my street—may they turn to you ....

Going Forward

Commit to a week of using car time as prayer pod time.
Or a month.
Or for the foreseeable future.
Thank you for partnering with God to bring his kingdom into this world.

PRAYER REFRESH 17

GROANING PRAYER

Prayer doesn't always need words. For some of the deepest suffering, a groan might be all you can manage—and that's okay, too.

Some years ago, a friend of ours was involved in a bitter divorce battle that dragged on for years. I never knew the details, except the day before his final court date, we got word that the situation seemed hopeless. A hostile judge. A former wife who seemed to be able to lie with impunity.

I had no words. I literally could just groan—deep moans from the gut.

Our friend's court date the next day turned out to be in his favor.

It was a miracle.

Surprise! I didn't actually need words.

Paul says, "The Spirit helps us in our weakness. For we do not know what to pray for as we ought, but the Spirit himself intercedes for us with groanings too deep for words."[25]

Refresh

Think of something that seems so big, so impossible, so hopeless that you can hardly pray for.

Groan about it.

Lord, this situation is so complex, I have no words.

Going Forward

Don't forget this type of prayer! Some things in life hurt almost like childbirth. When you can't form words, it's okay to simply groan before God.

As a believer in Christ, you are not left on your own. The Lord sends his great advantage, the Holy Spirit, to help you. He hears your sighs. He hears your groans. He is with you.

PRAY FOR A RANDOM FRIEND

When a random person comes to mind—like an almost forgotten childhood friend, or a person you once saw on a plane—pray for that person.

When I was a girl, I mentioned to my mom that sometimes someone would pop into my mind that I hadn't thought of in years.

She said, "Maybe you should pray for those people—maybe the Lord is bringing them to mind."

What a lovely thought!

I try to remember that suggestion. Sometimes the person who comes to mind isn't even a friend, but a random person I briefly talked to in the airport, or a person I once saw on the bus.

For a long time, I had no proof that these random promptings were from God. But still ... I figured that prayer is good. And I like the verse in the Amplified Bible that says the Holy Spirit "dwells within you [directs and controls you]."[26]

Then, one day, I had proof!

I transferred schools a few times in high school. I had a friend from the first school who had been very dear to me, but I hadn't kept up with her.

Fifteen years or so after I knew her, she suddenly came to mind a few times in the course of a day or two. I prayed a blessing over her and went on with my day.

The next week, the newspaper reported a challenging situation for her family.

I grieved for my friend.

I was also so touched that the Lord cared enough for her to give her extra prayer coverage.

And I was humbled to be that prayer coverage.

So pray for those random people who come to mind! That's the prompting of the Holy Spirit!

Refresh

Ask God, "What unexpected person would you have me pray for?" Pray for that person.

If God also gives you a specific request—fantastic. Otherwise, you can pray a blessing over them, and that they would come to know God in a deeper way.

Lord God, thank you for that former coworker who was such a pleasure to work with. I pray that you would guide, direct, and bless him, wherever he is in life. Thank you that you connect your people. Please make me attentive to your direction. If I'm not paying attention, please be a little louder. Thank you for your patience with my slow ears.

Going Forward

Start to pay attention and pray for anyone who randomly comes to mind.

This doesn't just have to apply to the almost-forgotten, of

course. If you know a friend has a doctor's appointment, you can pray for your friend when the need comes to mind. (When it comes to mind right at the time the appointment is set to start, that's really exciting!)

This is a fun exercise, because we always have memories randomly come to mind. And those around us can always use prayer.

PRAYER REFRESH 19

PRAY THE PRAYERS OF PAUL

**Paul fills his epistles with the prayers
of his heart for his fellow believers.**

Pray continually.[27]

In the past, I have used Paul's instruction for self-flagellation. I can track whole years with little prayer—hardly a shining example of "pray continually."

And I have definitely struggled with "Rejoice evermore."

But I've changed my mind about Paul. N.T. Wright's amazing *Paul: A Biography* brought Paul to a more human scale for me. What love he had for the saints! What assurance to ask for bold things! What intimacy with God!

Zealous, brilliant, sometimes rejoicing, occasionally despairing. A man who loved Jesus, who faced rejection and betrayal, who poured out his life, and saw fruitfulness and disappointment both.

Through it all, he was a man of prayer, and he repeatedly encouraged his churches and his friends to pray.

And his prayers! Amazing. What love he had for the saints! What assurance to ask for bold things! What intimacy with God!

He asked for big things, with expectation that those prayers would be answered.

His prayers offer a whole new level of prayer training.

Refresh

Pray this prayer over yourself, taken from Colossians 1:9–14. Speak these words of hope over yourself. This was Paul's prayer for believers, so I trust that it applies equally to you and me as it did to the first century Christians.

God, I ask you to fill me with the knowledge of your will through all the wisdom and understanding that the Spirit gives, so that I may live a life worthy of Jesus and please him in every way: bearing fruit in every good work, growing in the knowledge of you, being strengthened with all power according to your glorious might so that I may have great endurance and patience, and give joyful thanks to you, Father, as you have qualified me and this generation of believers to share in the inheritance of your holy people in the kingdom of light. For you, God, have rescued us from the dominion of darkness and brought us into the kingdom of the Son you love, in whom we have redemption, the forgiveness of sins.

Going Forward

Pray the prayers of Paul until they become part of your natural pattern of prayer.

Here are several references you can pursue.

- I Corinthians 1:4–9
- II Corinthians 1:3–7
- Ephesians 1:3–23
- Ephesians 3:14–21
- Philippians 1:3–11
- I Thessalonians 3:9–13

And may you celebrate that you are in the kingdom of light.

PRAYERS TO REMEMBER GOD'S PRESENCE

Want significant life transformation? Start to remember God's presence throughout the day.

Several saints through the ages have written about their desire to remain constantly connected with God. Brother Lawrence, a monk who lived in the 1600s, explained in *The Practice of the Presence of God* how he would try to constantly remember God. "I cannot imagine how religious persons can live satisfied without the practice of the presence of God."

"We should establish ourselves in a sense of God's presence, by continually conversing with Him."

"Think often on God, by day, by night, in your business and even in your diversions. He is always near you and with you; leave him not alone."

Evelyn Christenson, in *What Happens When Women Pray*, described this connection as a time when you're sitting before a fire with a loved one. You don't need to talk all the time to assure the other person you're still there and engaged. The line of communication is open, but it doesn't need to be used all the time.[28] So share the good things (or the less good things) as you go about your day.

Corrie ten Boom described her father like this: "Father would begin to pray with his friends in an attitude that was so easy and natural that the conversation never seemed to stop; it would flow easily from friend to friend to the Lord."[29]

More recently, Frank Laubach came up with the "game with minutes." Laubach suggested that believers see how many times in an hour they could turn their attention to God. Not as a stress thing, or a pressure thing, but as an opportunity to be closer to God.

He recommended that you could start playing during church. You're sitting there for an hour or two, after all. How many of those minutes can you turn your thoughts to God, even for one second?

Current research shows that gamification—turning everything into a game—keeps the brain engaged. Laubach was on to something!

My friend Carla Pratico, when she met God in a bar in her early twenties, wanted to remind herself that God was close to her. So she set a silent vibrate reminder on her phone for every ten minutes during her waking hours. Whether she was sitting in a meeting or talking to a friend or getting some food, six times an hour she would have a reminder of God's presence. When it went off, she would take a second and turn her affections to the Lord: "Thank you for your presence." It could last less than a second, but it helped her to be aware of her connection to God, helped to train her brain to always be thinking of God. "You can't be disconnected from God; he's connected to you, and his mind is made up. We get the opportunity to be aware of our union."

After a month, this had become her habit.

"The Lord replied, 'My Presence will go with you, and I will give you rest.'"[30]

Refresh

How can you keep your lines of communication open with God?

Lord, I want to walk with you more closely. Thank you for your presence.

Going Forward

This is an ongoing experiment. You get to walk with God more closely for the rest of your life. What a gift!

PRAYER REFRESH 21

BLESSING PRAYER

Receive blessing. Give blessing.

At a prayer conference, Cheryl Williams told of how she once had a conversation with the director of a drug rehab facility. The director said, "You know, we've never had a Jewish boy come through here."

Cheryl suspected that was because Jewish fathers place their hands on their sons' heads and bless them.

Growing up, my dad would pray the Aaronic blessing[31] over me and my siblings each night.

He added on a bit at the end that isn't in Numbers 6:24–26.

"The Lord bless you and keep you; the Lord make his face to shine upon you and be gracious to you; the Lord lift up his countenance upon you and give you peace, through Jesus Christ our Lord and our Savior."

Whenever guests leave the farm, I sing Michael Card's version "Barocha" over them (several versions available online).

So, since that's my tradition, I leave you with this.

Refresh

Please receive this blessing.

The LORD bless you and keep you.
The LORD make his face shine upon you
And give you peace,
And give you peace,
And give you peace forever.

The LORD be gracious to you.
The LORD turn his face towards you.
And give you peace,
And give you peace,
And give you peace forever.

Going Forward

Look for places where you can bless others.

You can start with a prayer as easy as, "May the Lord bless you."

And may the Lord, indeed, bless you!

NOTES

1 Carter, Pete, Dr. *Unwrapping Lzaraus*, 45
2 Exodus 32:11–14
3 Ephesians 6:17
4 John 10:27
5 https://youtu.be/ZAO8kiY6TLk
6 Luke 11:1
7 Travis, Chris. *InSignificant*. 88
8 James 1:17
9 *Seven Secrets to Power Praying*
10 Romans 6:12–14, *The Kingdom New Testament translation by N.T. Wright*
11 *Tramp for the Lord*, 55
12 I Peter 5:8, emphasis mine
13 Psalm 19:14
14 Mark 10:47–52
15 From Philippians 4:13
16 From Psalm 68:19
17 From Deuteronomy 28:6
18 From Nehemiah 8:10
19 From 2 Timothy 1:7
20 From 2 Corinthians 9:8
21 From Proverbs 16:7
22 From Zephaniah 3:17
23 From Psalm 103:4
24 From 1 Peter 2:24
25 Romans 8:26
26 Romans 8:9
27 I Thessalonians 5:17
28 P. 89
29 *In My Father's House*, 65
30 Exodus 33:14
31 Numbers 6:24-26

ABOUT THE AUTHOR

A.J. Lykosh loves healing and deliverance.

Her heart's cry comes from the verse, "My people are destroyed for lack of knowledge" (Hosea 4:6). The author of several highly acclaimed books, she seeks to stop the destruction as best she can through writing and speaking. She sends daily emails about prayer, and podcasts at Make Prayer Beautiful.

She loves feedback. Email amy@workplaceprayer.com to start a conversation.

MAKARIOS
PRESS
Be in your happy place.

PRAY HEAVEN
TO EARTH
Why Workplace Prayer Exists

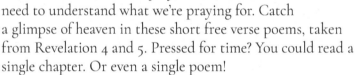

When Jesus taught on prayer, he began, "Our Father in heaven, hallowed be your name, your kingdom come, your will be done, on earth as it is in heaven." How can we effectively pray God's kingdom on earth, if we don't know what heaven looks like? If we want to pray better, we need to understand what we're praying for. Catch a glimpse of heaven in these short free verse poems, taken from Revelation 4 and 5. Pressed for time? You could read a single chapter. Or even a single poem!

> "I just sat down with your book. I am on the second page. In tears. Thank you. Beautiful and song-like. And fun." — **Sarah**

> "I feel like each line of each poem is like a choice morsel of truth that I just want to savor slowly. I set aside your book to read in quiet and cozy moments wrapped in a quilt on my bed. It is something I look forward to and cherish." — **Elena**

> "I love the short meditative chapters. It's great bedtime reading. Congratulations!!" — **Perry Marshall**

FIND OUT MORE AT
makariospress.com/heaven

THE PRINCE PROTECTS HIS CITY
Nehemiah Prayed Four Months, Then Rebuilt the Wall in Only 52 Days

A free verse look at the book of Nehemiah. Come meet a man who brought God's kingdom to bear in his work. Nehemiah wasn't a warrior or a king. He was a tremendous administrator, a gifted leader, a world-class historian, a treasured friend, a successful fund-raiser, and a prince. And he prayed constantly.

"Loved it. Such a nice quick pace to read Nehemiah and also space to sit in parts if I just wanted to read one page" — **Angela**

**FIND OUT MORE AT
amazon.com**

ONE VOICE: THE STORY OF WILLIAM WILBERFORCE
Gorgeous Story of Tenacity + Courage

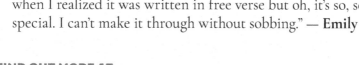

Biography in verse of the man who, despite all obstacles, fought to end the Slave Trade in Great Britain. Powerful story of tenacity and courage.

"One Voice has become one of my absolute favourite books of all time. I was so skeptical when I realized it was written in free verse but oh, it's so, so special. I can't make it through without sobbing." — **Emily**

**FIND OUT MORE AT
sonlight.com**

Made in USA - Kendallville, IN
38501_9781956561036
02.02.2023 1653